The
Genealogical Proof Standard
and
French Genealogy
Second edition

FGB

Anne Morddel

Suggested library cataloguing:

Morddel, Anne
    The Genealogical Proof Standard and French Genealogy, 2nd edition

    Summary: Practical advice on applying the American genealogical proof standard to the customs, practices and documentation of French genealogy.

[1. Genealogy. 2. France - History.] I. Title

ISBN 979-10-96085-00-2

Table of Contents

Introduction

This booklet contains eleven posts from the first seven years of "The French Genealogy Blog"[1] on the subject of the largely American Genealogical Proof Standard as it may be applied to the documentation found in French genealogy. Most of these posts were written during our participation in a study group on the book by Thomas W. Jones entitled "Mastering Genealogical Proof". At the time of going to press, the sessions of that study group could still be seen on YouTube.

This booklet follows on our first publication "French Genealogy From Afar"[2], which explains the basics of French genealogy and without which this booklet may seem a bit confusing. It is our most sincere wish that you, Dear Reader, would find it of use when it comes to analyzing and evaluating the results of your French genealogical research.

---

[1] http://french-genealogy.typepad.com/genealogie/

[2] like this booklet, available from www.lulu.com

Part One

As most of our Dear Readers in the United States will already know, the genealogy community there is abuzz with discussions of the recent publication, "Mastering Genealogical Proof", by Thomas W. Jones, published by the National Genealogical Society[3]. This is the latest publication in a long and laudable effort begun some years ago by Elizabeth Shown Mills and others to raise the standards of genealogical research in that country from the erratic to the reliable and even scholarly.

On the grounds that one can never study too often or learn too much, we bought the book and planned to read it diligently. On the grounds that isolated study produces a lunatic solipsist, we sought a study group online and found two people offering such, though there may be more, Angela McGhie[4] and Pat Richley-Erickson[5], of "Dear Myrtle" renown. On the grounds of the insurmountability of sleepiness and failure of concentration due to time differences between continents, we chose the latter, which records the discussions on YouTube[6] and to which we listen during civilized hours. Finally, on the grounds that the principles described and recommended in "Mastering Genealogical Proof" may present a conundrum or two when applied to French genealogical documentation and research, we thought that we might share our more lucid thoughts and ever strong opinions on those conundrums with you, Dear Readers, as we follow the online meetings of this study group.

The first meeting was merely the nuts and bolts of "orientation" and a discussion of the author's Preface; the second began the study with Chapter One. That chapter

---

[3] http://www.ngsgenealogy.org/cs/mastering_genealogical_proof

[4] http://genealogyeducation.blogspot.fr

[5] http://blog.dearmyrtle.com

[6] https://www.youtube.com/watch?v=HwXZk-HMuNQ

gives definitions: of genealogy and of the proof standard, as codified by the Board for Certification of Genealogists.[7] The five elements of the proof standard are:

- Reasonably exhaustive search
- Complete and accurate citation of sources
- Analysis and correlation of the collected information
- Resolution of conflicting evidence.
- Soundly reasoned, coherently written conclusion.

The discussion included the somewhat flabbergasting question "Does the pursuit of genealogy (or family history) for pleasure obviate the need for accuracy?" To us, and we were relieved to see that to most others, accurate genealogy presents facts, possibly even truth, while inaccurate genealogy presents not fiction, for fiction is clearly identified as an imagined account, but falseness as it is presented as factual when it is not. We were most staggered to hear that some of the participants felt that the fun of genealogical research would be lost if accuracy were required.

This little part of the discussion sheds light not only on the urgent need for this textbook, but on one of the essential differences between the historical practice of genealogy in France versus that in the United States. In the United States, genealogy began as something of a hobby, and became more popular with the creation of lineage societies. As Ms. Richley-Erickson stated during the discussion, she had once known someone who had said something along the lines of: "I don't care who my ancestors really were, I just want to get into the DAR." For some, it is also an aspect of the practice of their religion. Loosely quoting Ms. Richley-Erikson again: "As a good Mormon girl, I did genealogy." While genealogy continues to be a pastime for

[7] http://www.bcgcertification.org

most, the quality of the research and reports is being held to ever higher standards of accuracy.

In France, however, genealogy as a pastime is a recent development, though genealogical research has existed for centuries. Before the Revolution, being able to prove one's lineage was not only for the aristocracy but could be vital in matters of inheritance and/or tax relief. While one now rarely can hope for tax relief because of one's ancestors, genealogy is still quite relevant to inheritance. There are, today, two types of genealogical research recognized in France:

- *généalogie successorale* - this is similar to probate genealogy in that some of the focus is on finding heirs, but it extends much further into identifying ancestors as well because for over two hundred years French law has required that heirs of up to the sixth degree of kinship must be sought. The *généalogiste successoral* is not trained in the profession at any university but goes through training on the job in an office of professional genealogists, who are quite competitive and who have large genealogical indices of their own. Additionally the professional genealogist researching an heir has access to the more recent civil registrations and census returns, which the family genealogist does not, as they are protected by privacy laws. Such genealogists work not only with *notaires* but with insurers and the Land Registry; and their research and reports must be able to stand up in a court of law. He or she tends to sneer at the family historian, who may merely be seeking more attendees for the family reunion, or *cousinade*.

- *généalogie familiale* - is the practice of researching one's family history to discover one's ancestors and to learn more about their lives. In France, this is a relatively new phenomenon that became extraordinarily popular in the latter part of the twentieth century.

Thus, the practice of genealogy in France has been held to rigorous standards from its inception. To be sure, frauds have existed, but sloppiness and inaccuracy have never been the norm. That there are now considered to be two pursuits with the same name is something that has caused great annoyance to those in the first category. However, those in the second category most certainly emulate the high standards of *généalogie successorale*.

We will be continuing to follow this fine study group and to share our reflections on it and on "Mastering Genealogical Proof " in relation to French Genealogy.

Part Two

The second chapter of "Mastering Genealogical Proof" deals with definitions and categorizations: of source, of the information sources contain, and of the genealogical evidence that can be drawn from the information. It agrees with Chapter One of Elizabeth Shown Mills's "Evidence Explained"[8], but for the addition of the category of "indeterminable information", e.g. that which appears in a source, apparently out of the blue and certainly unattributably.

We read the chapter. We did the homework and are ashamed to say that our scribbles for that, wending their way around the margins, looked about the same as they did when we were a tot in school. We listened to Dear Myrtle's discussion group and panel on Chapter Two. There, we were told of an interview with the book's author, Thomas W. Jones, on the Blog Talk Radio's "The Forget-Me-Not Hour" by Jane Wilcox, so we listened to that too. (And, life on the Internet being such as it is, we also wandered off topic to watch Neymar and Fred knock out Spain in the Confederations Cup. How we should love to see the beautiful game triumph once again over the coarse, "go for injury" form the game takes in Europe.... The children call this Jackson Pollock style of concentration "multi-tasking".)

As we read the chapter and listened to the discussion and interview, we realized that the application of the categories of information to French documentation is in some ways much easier and in others a bit tougher. The essential differences between French documentation and American records (the latter being the focus of the book), aside from language, are two:

---

[8] https://www.evidenceexplained.com

- Civil, as opposed to parish or religious, documentation in America went from almost nothing in the earlier years to documents with an increasing amount of information. In many places, birth, marriage and death records were not kept until the mid-nineteenth century. Remoter places without churches or other religious establishments had no parish records either. While in France, in spite of a few revolutions, there has been a steady recording of births or baptisms, marriages and deaths or burials since the sixteenth century.

- In America, each state, once it decided to record information about individuals, determined what to record and how. There can be at least fifty different types of birth registration, and many more when the differences at the county level are taken into consideration. In France, the department is merely an administrative division, not a separate state with its own rights that is part of a federation. France is a republic with one and only one government, directed from Paris and the directives carried out at the departmental, *arrondissement* and town levels throughout the country. Thus, all civil registrations at any one time follow the same format. Historically and still today, that format for a civil registration generally contains a great deal more information than a civil registration does in America.

This means that a researcher in America has to deal with a lack of civil registration that must be supplemented with other types of documentation (such as tax records, court records, etc.) and that much of the documentation, especially if it were created in a remote area with little administration, may not be trustworthy. Thus, much of the emphasis of the Genealogical Proof Standard is on the quality of the source and the source of the information. In France, however, civil and legal documentation tends to be more trustworthy for the simple reason that one always has had to show a document to make a document, e.g. to show an authenticated and official copy of one's birth registration or baptism registration (or now, one's identity card) to enroll in the army or to marry.

Primary, Secondary and Indeterminable Information

This requirement enhances the trustworthiness of French documentation -- by the criteria under discussion -- significantly. One panellist, Kathryn Lake Hogan, recounted a tale of a man who, on applying for a marriage license, gave an incorrect name for his parent. This would be unimaginable in France as both of the couple must present official copies of their birth registrations in order to marry, and those birth registrations give their parents' full names.

Just after that (at about one hour and eight minutes on the counter) moderator Myrtle asked the panellists if any of them could think of a source that contained more than one of the types of information, being primary, secondary or indeterminable. We would suggest that information of an indeterminable source (coming from an informant that cannot be determined as either primary or secondary) would occur rarely if ever in French documentation and that most French documentation would be a mix of primary and secondary information.

The French marriage registration of the nineteenth century exemplifies a source with mixed categories of primary and secondary information. The standard format contains the following information:

1. The date, time and full location (*commune, canton, arrondissement* and *département*) as written by the officer recording the event, as well as his full name, honours and title. (This can often be the lengthiest part of the registration, providing little genealogical information, unless one is researching the officer's family.)

2. The full name and title of the groom, his profession, his residence, if he is living with his parents or not, if

he is of the age of majority or not, his date and place of birth, the full names of his parents, their professions and whether they are living or not. If a parent has died, the date and place of death will also be given. Whether or not a parent is present will be stated and if not, why not. Whether or not the parents give their consent to the marriage will also be stated.

3. The same information as for the groom will be given for the bride.

4. The dates and locations of the posting of the banns and whether or not that resulted in anyone opposing the marriage.

5. Possibly, there will be a statement as to if there were a marriage contract.

6. Confirmation that the marriage section of the *Code Civil* was read to the couple and that they agreed to it, both verbally and by signing the register, and that they were thus as married, their names being given again.

7. The names, professions, ages, addresses and relationship to the couple of the witnesses.

8. Signatures or marks of all those named: the officer, the couple, their parents or guardians, the witnesses.

The primary information in the above would be numbers:

- 1, for the officer is giving the date and location and information about himself

- 4, either partially or completely, for the banns would have been posted in the place of residence of each of the couple, at least one of whom would have lived in the place where the marriage was performed. Thus, the same officer would have posted the banns of at least one of the couple, making this information primary. If the other of the couple lived elsewhere, the banns would have been posted there as well and this reported to the officer, making the information secondary

- 6, for the officer recording the marriage is also the one performing it
- The signatures

The secondary information would be numbers:

- 2, for though the groom is present, with his parents, and though he has presented a copy of his birth registration and, if a parent has died, a copy of the death registration, the person recording that information is the officer
- 3, for the same reasons as above
- 5, for if there were a marriage contract, in order for the regime it specified to cover the marriage, the officer would have had to have seen only the proof of its having been registered, not the contract itself
- 7, for again, the officer is recording what the witnesses tell of themselves, even if they have to present forms of identification

Obviously, because of the documentation that would have been presented to the officer, and because of the presence of the couple, their parents and their family, much of the secondary information is nearly as good as primary. If, as sometimes occurred, one or both of the couple were born in the commune where they married, the officer may have been in the same post at that time and may have been the recorder of their birth in the register, which would make much of the information in numbers 2 and 3 primary.

Vagueness and lies are rare in French civil registrations. False documentation is almost non-existent, (though we have heard tell of a baron who, on divorcing his wife, rather inconsiderately had fabricated a false *Livret de*

Famille or Family Book, containing no children when in truth he had four; it was a crime of passion that fooled no one). Finally, primary and secondary information often occur in the same source.

Part Three

The third chapter of "Mastering Genealogical Proof" discusses Thorough Research, the first element of the Genealogical Proof Standard. Dr. Jones seems to be writing as if dealing with a strange batch of researchers who have asked "How much is enough?", a question that can stem only from those who are either

- Confused about conclusions that can be drawn reasonably from a body of evidence with those that must be absolute, indisputable and unchangeable TRUTH, or
- Lazy

To our mind, thorough research means identifying, locating and examining all possible resources, being perfectly aware that many will be missed, making it an ongoing process, followed by a phase of analysis during which it is discovered that most of what was found cannot be used. Dr. Jones gives six criteria for this process, putting the reduction at the beginning.

The discussion of Chapter Three on Dear Myrtle's MPS Study Group went over the above points and spent much time on Dr. Jones's terms and definitions, as well as on the value of different types of sources. None of these concepts would be very different in relation to French genealogical records. One obvious difference in Chapter Three, however, is the Table of "Suggestions for Identifying Sources to Answer Genealogical Questions" (page 25) for it covers sources of use mostly to those researching ancestors in the United States, such as the National Genealogical Society's "Research in the States" series.

After about the first hour of the online discussion, there was some talk of the directive by Dr. Jones that "authored, derivative works must be replaced by originals and primary information." We cannot stress this enough when it comes to those early twentieth century, American authored works about French records. They were usually written with glory in mind and with qualifying for membership in a lineage society as the motive. In nine cases out of ten, it is our experience that, while their research in American records may be exemplary, as to French records they simply cannot be trusted.

The most extreme case came to us not long ago when *Madame B.* asked us to help verify claims made in a lineage file which she had purchased from an American lineage society (some of them, to their shame, sell photocopies of their members' application forms and supporting documentation without those members' consent). Written by one Leonardo Andrea, a well-known genealogist in his day, it made utterly false claims as to the French ancestry of a man named Peter LeBoon, who probably was French, and who died in South Carolina. We looked at the original parish registrations online and found that no date of birth, marriage or death, nor evidence of the family in the supposed town of origin (Rochefort) appeared. Not a single one of Andrea's claims -- and there were many -- about the man, his wife, his children or his parents could be verified in the parish registrations online on the website of the relevant Departmental Archives.

Andrea's sources for his French "facts" were almost all untrustworthy for they either had "disappeared" or were books to which he had written the relevant contribution, as in the case of "Old Southern Bible Records". Some sources seem to have been fabricated and certainly were not substantiated, such as a "war record" from France and a tombstone in Rochefort. In fact, the entirety of the French ancestry seems to have been fabricated, though this has not prevented its being spread all over the Internet, of course. Clearly, Andrea and others of his club never imagined that their work concerning French documentation could or would be checked. We find the cynicism of such boldly told untruths perhaps no more than the lineage society deserved, but chilling nevertheless.

We cannot urge you enough, Dear Readers, never to trust lineage society files, insofar as they concern French genealogy, and to check -- as Dr. Jones suggests -- every fact gleaned from every authored, derivative work.

Part Four

We write during a *canicule*, defined as a heat wave during which the temperature never goes below twenty degrees Celsius, not even at night. Fortunately, we are blessed with a country home of stone in which the ground floor -- where we are at the moment -- never has a temperature higher than twenty-five degrees, even during a *canicule* such as this when just now, the temperature on the other side of the door in the blazing afternoon sun is thirty-eight. We shall do our best not to become addled.

The fourth chapter of Jones's "Mastering Genealogical Proof" is one we have been reading with some interest, for it covers the procedures for and elements of proper citations of sources, with reference to Elizabeth Shown Mills's "Evidence Explained", the definitive work on the subject for genealogists in North America. Dr. Jones writes that every citation must contain at last five elements of information (which we paraphrase freely here):

- Who was the source's author or creator or, to be anthropological, informant?
- What is the source, e.g. its title and, if necessary further identification?
- When was the source created?
- Where in the source is located the piece of information being used, e.g page number or entry number?
- Where is the source itself located?

To our mind, the two reasons for citation of information sources are:

- To prove that, unlike Leonardo Andrea, you did not simply make it up; or plagiarize it, and
- To enable those who read your work to find for themselves the source and information that you quote.

Thus, a good citation is a set of identifiers that serve as directions for someone who may not know the source at all to be able to find it and then to find the very piece of information in it that you used. If they cannot, your citation is not good enough.

As citing pertains to French records, we have for some time been mulling over the recommendations given in "Evidence Explained" and have some questions. We would like to elucidate some of our points here:

- It seems to us that it would be better not to give English titles for French records, except perhaps in parentheses, if desired. If, for example, a source is given as "French census of 1911" instead of *"Dénombrement de 1911 - Liste Nominative"*, you only make it more difficult for the person who wishes to find the source you have listed, especially if you are citing a French website.
- The same holds true for sections of records, column headings, etc. They should be given as they appear, in French. Translations should appear, if at all, in parentheses. Again, someone looking at a French census return, will not want to have to look up the possible words for household, but should be told that the column heading is *"ménage"* from the start. By giving what is on the record, possibilities for confusion are reduced.

- In citing jurisdiction, we had thought that all of the above should be given, with the addition of the unique INSEE code for the *commune* (see Appendix A). This would allow for the shorter citation to give only the *commune* with the INSEE code and the *Département*. However, most French archivists feel that this is not necessary. (See Appendix B)

- The recording of births or baptisms, marriages and deaths or burials in France can seem confusing but is not. Essentially:

    - Baptisms, marriages and burials performed by a priest or pastor were recorded in parish registers which are called *registres paroissiaux*. After 1792, and the separation of church and state, though parish registrations continued to be and still are recorded, they are no longer required by law, nor are they considered to be a legal record about a person.

    - Parish registrations were copied or often written anew by a clerk, or *greffier*; this copy was **contemporary** and was signed by the same people who signed the parish registration. This copy was held in local administrative offices.

    - Both copies of parish registrations recorded before 1792 were placed under the authority of the state and ordered to be sent to the newly created Departmental Archives. (This is murky. Originally, according to Gildas Bernard[9], p. 35, the church copy went to the Town Hall or *Mairie*, and the clerk's, or *greffier's*, copy to the Departmental Archives; now, however, many of the Departmental

---

[9] Bernard, Gildas. *Guide des recherches sur l'histoire des familles.* Paris : Archives nationales, 1981.

Archives have both copies.) Churches, parish archives and diocesan archives do not hold any parish registrations prior to 1792 (well, some cheated, but most did not) but they **do** hold parish registrations after that date to the present. So far as we can determine, when the Church of Jesus Christ of Latter-day Saints (Mormons) filmed French parish registrations, they filmed only one copy, the ecclesiastical copy and not the copy made by the clerk. However, Departmental Archives are now filming the clerk's copies and putting them on their websites. (The slight differences between the two make this useful to the genealogist.)

- From 1792, civil registrations, known as acts, were mandated to record births, marriages and deaths. They are called *acte de naissance*, *acte de mariage* and *acte de décès*. These are the rough equivalent of what are known as vital records in the United States. These were recorded in register books by the *officier d'état civil*. In a small *commune*, that function will be fulfilled by the mayor; in a large city, an *officier d'état civil* will be employed. *Actes d'état civil* are created in duplicate. One copy is sent, at regular intervals, often of ten years, to the Departmental Archives. One copy remains in the Town Hall, or *Mairie*.

- In citing parish and civil registrations, no standard English or French term should be used. We suggest that the French title of the particular register or film seen is what should be given. Sometimes, register books held all three types of registration intermingled, as they were written chronologically. Sometimes, births and marriages were in one register and deaths in another. Sometimes, each type had its own register. This is clearly identified in the title given on any digital version on a Departmental Archive website. To use a generic term will only create confusion, especially as the duplicate registers begin to appear among the lists.

- Following on from the above, the copy used, whether the clerk's the priest's or the mayor's, must be specified. As to which set is original, which a copy, which contains primary information and which secondary, we would suggest that, if the record contains the participants' signatures, there is a good chance that it contains primary information.

- We would warn against using a website page as the website identification. The ultimate home page should be, we suggest, the website cited. At times, this may be a Departmental Archives website but it may also be a general Departmental website, with the archives section having a sub-page, along with sports, libraries, taxes, and other local administrative activities.

We are aware that the many citation formats within genealogy software programmes do not really support full citation of French documentation, as per our suggestions. This means that many would have to be crafted in the category of "free form" or its equivalent, which is a bore, to be sure. However, if the goal is clarity, there may be no other choice.

Part Five

We continue to swelter, with daily temperatures hovering at forty-four degrees Celsius. Days are spent in darkened rooms, working quietly, waiting for the fiercely blazing sun to set. Evenings have been a joy of late, spent with a delightful group of you, Dear Readers, who have come all this way to our patch of the French countryside to chat late into the night about their French genealogy research and brick walls. They have shared some fascinating puzzles and challenges about which we hope to write here anon.

While in our darkened, somewhat cooler rooms, we have been carrying on with our participation after the fact in Dear Myrtle's Study Group on "Mastering Genealogical Proof" by Thomas W. Jones. We have been finding the contributions of Carol Kostakos Petranek to be particularly lucid, and her sharing of her experience in researching European records (Greek and Polish) to have some occasional relevance to French research.

Chapter Five is about using the differentiations learned in Chapter Three to analyze and correlate the information. There are recommendations as to how to do that, with some excellent charts and tables as examples for organizing information. There is little in this crucial process that would be different when applied to French records.

Some of the discussion did highlight how important it is to clear one's mind of prejudices and assumptions when analyzing and correlating. One must leave aside every belief, hope, fear, suspicion, prejudice, dream, assumption and so forth held about the people and lives under scrutiny. Stop suspecting pre-marital sex every time a child is born less than nine months after a marriage, stop suspecting bigamy, stop suspecting false identity, false parents and false ages, stop hoping for nobility or a connection to celebrity. While any of that may turn out to be the case later, it is catastrophic to the process to have such assumptions or suspicions in mind at the time of analysis for they will becloud vision.

One must have the clarity and observational habits of the scientific researcher who with a pure celibacy of mind sees only what is there and not what he or she desires to see. (For a most elegant example of such clarity, we recommend Darwin's "Voyage of the Beagle".) One must expect nothing but note everything. Only then will rational analysis and correlation - with French information or any other -- be possible.

So much of "Mastering Genealogical Proof" and the discussion of it dwells upon the problems of American documentation of record keeping having arrived late and of people having taken advantage of officials' somewhat minimalist approach to creating early vital records. As we have stated many times before, this is not the case with the French parish and civil registrations. From 1792, the *Code Civil* has outlined for all of France exactly what is to be written for each of the three civil registrations and it has varied little over the last two centuries. As the birth registration, the *acte de naissance*, is so important, we give here some key points from Chapter Two of the original *Code Civil* as to how it must be completed:

- A birth declaration must be made within three days of the birth (allowances of a day are made for Sundays and holidays) to the registrar of civil registrations (the *officier d'état civil*) of the place where the birth occurred AND the child must be presented to the registrar. (Article 55) Any attempt to register a birth more than three days after the child was born requires court approval from the court having jurisdiction in the place where the child was born.

- The declaration of the birth must be made by the father. If he is not present, it must be made by the person who assisted at the birth, e.g. doctor, midwife, health officer, etc.; AND where the birth was outside the residence of the mother, by the head of the household where she gave birth. (Article 56)

- The birth registration must be completed immediately, in the presence of two witnesses. (Article 56)
- The birth registration MUST include: the day, the hour, and the place of birth, the sex of the child, the names given to the child, the full names of the parents and their professions and address, also the full names, professions and addresses of the two witnesses. (Article 57)

This was the standard format for all nineteenth and twentieth century birth registrations in all of France and remains the same today. Variations are few and slight. Changes have been minimal and the modern code is very similar to the original. To be sure, mistakes occurred, people lied, registrars were overworked or incompetent, but on the whole, a French birth registration is a document that can be trusted. Implicitly? Of course not; no source can be trusted implicitly.

Much Study Group discussion took place concerning the alteration and/or falsification of documents or parts of documents with the conclusion being that only unaltered documents may be considered reliable. This conclusion can be applied only partially to French civil registrations. Birth and marriage registrations are not altered but do have marginal notes added at later dates and these notes become part of the official record. This is particularly true of the birth registration.

In France, the birth registration serves as an official record of the registered events in the person's life. In the margin will be added the date and place of marriages, the names of spouses, the dates and places of any divorces, and the death of the subject of the registration. This additional information is received from the registrar who recorded it and then sent it to the registrar in the birthplace of the subject, to be added to the birth registration (making lies a bit more difficult). Unlike with American records, these alterations do not reduce but enhance the value of the record as a source.

Perhaps one of the most difficult categories explained by Dr. Jones is that of "related sources" -- those of which one is the source for the information in the other -- as opposed to "independent sources" -- those which were created without any reference to one another (page 59). Using this criterion, almost all French records would be related sources. This is because, knowing that the birth registration is so strictly created and updated, officials constantly require certified copies of it or of the portable family set of certified extracts of birth and death registrations, known as the *Livret de Famille*. For all of the following, one must present either one or the other:

- To obtain an Identity card
- For Registration in school
- For Registration in the military
- To be considered for honours such as the Légion d'Honneur
- To marry
- To register to vote
- To register for the census

Thus, from 1792 onwards in France, civil registrations, military records, electoral rolls, census returns, school records, identity documents and honorary society memberships must all be considered as "related sources".

Where to look for "independent sources"? Notarial records, land records and court records would be the first places to look, but any one of these could have used one of the above "related sources" -- all of them dependent upon the birth registration -- to confirm a person's identity.

One final difference between French birth registrations and those discussed in the Study Group: in the French birth registrations there would seem to be fewer lies than in the American version for the simple reason that the French allow a person to say nothing. There are innumerable birth registrations for a child who was presented to the registrar by a midwife or doctor and whose father and sometimes mother as well were "not named". There are many, many marriage registrations in which a parent to one of the couple is termed "absent, whereabouts unknown". This may have occurred even when everyone in town knew who the child's parents were; or even if the "absent" parent were standing right there at the marriage.

Why is this so? We can only guess: lying is considered a sin but silence is not, perhaps. Or perhaps, on the assumption that people will lie, silence is offered as an option to preserve the credibility of the system? Parental anonymity certainly is seen to save unwanted babies' lives. These are only guesswork. Sadly for family genealogists, these silences are usually the thickest and most solid of brick walls.

Part Six

Moving along at a snapping pace, we and Dear Myrtle's MPG Study Group have now reached Chapter Six of Dr. Thomas Jones's "Mastering Genealogical Proof". This chapter's lesson is a piece of cake to understand although the practice may not always to be so easy to follow well.

Entitled "Resolving Conflicts and Assembling Evidence", it is neatly straightforward in explaining how to work through the results of one's research with a clear head and to sort out contradictions with intellectual integrity. It is not that far removed from the "Reasoning" section of our children's Quickstudy pamphlet on Essays and Term Papers. (To be honest, an awful lot of Dr. Jones's book seems to be more about how to write a good term paper than about genealogical proof, which -- considering some of the "genealogies" we have seen over the years -- may not be a bad thing at all.)

As with the first component of the Genealogical Proof Standard -- thorough research -- this, the fourth component -- "resolution of any conflicts between evidence and the proposed answer to a research question" is a skill of intellectual rigour that does not vary, whether it be applied to evidence found in American, French or any other nationality of record. We cannot think of any situation in which one would use different conflict resolution standards because of a different language or nationality of documentation.

So, we think it might be more useful to tell of some of the types of conflicts we have encountered in working with French records, which are not many. The majority of conflicts we have found are between the French information about a person and the information found in the documents on that person in another country. In fact, these conflicts are so many and so creatively made that they do, at times, seem to have been intentional. In short, we are not the only one to have changed our name[10]. We have come across:

- A man who got on a ship in Le Havre in 1836 under one name and got off that ship in New Orleans under a new name. (Some years later, he had changed his race as well.) This would seem to fall into the category of one item of direct-evidence conflicting with another item of direct-evidence (using the terms on page 74) if (and this cannot be certain) it were the passenger who gave his name to the person creating the list at both departure and arrival.

- A man whom the family has always thought was a son of the immigrant couple, who went from Audincourt, France to Connecticut, but who turned out to be their grandson. This was a case of items of indirect-evidence and family stories in conflict with items of direct-evidence.

- A family who claim and have documents that seem to prove that their surname indicates descent from Native Americans but whose ancestors in France used the surname in notarial records a good dozen years before emigration, a case of items of direct-evidence in conflict with items of direct-evidence. (Thanks to *Madame M* for this example.)

There exists the possibility in French birth registration for a parent to refuse to be identified[11]; this has brought to our notice an odd conflict:

---

[10] See our booklet entitled "Identity Wars".

[11] *Accouchement sous X*, described in our book, "French Genealogy From Afar".

- A man for whom no documentation or evidence of any kind provides a link to a French aviator, but who has the same surname and -- in photographs -- apparently nearly all of the same genes, a case of items of negative-evidence in conflict with niggling suspicions, leading nowhere but intriguing nevertheless.

A number of foreigners seem to have been aware of this possibility of silence in French birth registration and appear to have come to France specifically to take advantage of it, leading to cases of items of direct-evidence in conflict with negative evidence :

- Quite a few cases of a child and mother turning up in a British census around the time of the child's first birthday. The census gives their nationality as British, and the child's place of birth as France, but no record of birth for a child of that name can be found.
- A couple claiming to have been married in South Carolina were parents of a child born in Marseilles, but no US documentation supporting the marriage can be found. (Thanks to *Monsieur C* for this example.)

On a final note, though this did not come up in the discussion on Chapter Six, but we like very much Dr. Jones's comment that "Not all conflicting evidence can be resolved." How we wish more people would simply accept this and not try to force documentation to say what it does not!

Part Seven

What with one thing and another, we have fallen a tad behind Dear Myrtle's MPG Study Group on Dr. Thomas Jones's "Mastering Genealogical Proof". They discussed Chapter Seven a couple of weeks ago and we come to it here only now.

In truth, there is little of urgency. Chapter Seven discusses how to write a Genealogical Proof Summary, giving formats so exquisitely precise and clear that one could almost call them templates. Many of those on Dear Myrtle's discussion panel and those listeners writing in their comments, as well as Dear Myrtle herself pointed out that this was not so much a lesson in genealogy or research but one in how to write clearly and communicate one's proof well. Naturally, the entire chapter also applies to a Genealogical Proof Summary using evidence taken from French sources; foreign sources are no excuse for logic and clarity to tumble by the wayside.

What we may be able to contribute by way of suggestion or assistance toward maintaining a pristine style when using French sources could come only from our own guide. We use two books, both by the inestimable Fowler (with his brother in one case and a modernizing editor in another): "A Dictionary of Modern English Usage"[1] and "The King's English"[2]. Generally, we follow him to the letter, though there are times when our native recalcitrance will send us on a little spree of stubborn adherence to a practice he disdains. His advice on French usage could be quite handy to those of you writing up a Genealogical Proof Summary based on dozens of *actes d'état civil, recensements* and French notarial records.

Some of Fowler's gems:

French Words: "Display of superior knowledge is as great a vulgarity as display of superior wealth -- greater indeed, inasmuch as knowledge should tend more definitely than wealth towards discretion and good manners. That is the guiding principle alike in the using and pronouncing of

French words in English writing and talk. To use French words that your reader or hearer does not know or does not fully understand.....as if you were one of the select few to whom French is second nature when he is not one of those few (and it is ten thousand to one that neither you nor he will be) is inconsiderate and rude." (Dictionary, p. 212)

"Every writer who suspects himself [of wanting to use many French words]...should...remember that acquisitiveness and indiscriminate display are pleasing to contemplate only in birds and savages and children." (Dictionary, p. 212)

Foreign Words: "The usual protest must be made, to be treated no doubt with the usual disregard. The difficulty is that French, Latin, and other words are now also English, though the fiction that they are not is still kept up by italics and (with French words) conscientious efforts at pronunciation....To say *distrait* instead of *absent* or *absent-minded*, *bien entendu* for *of course*, *sans* for *without* ... *quand même* for *anyhow*, *penchant* for *liking* or *fancy*, *premier* for *first*, *coûte que coûte* for *at all costs*.....is pretension and nothing else." (King's English, pp. 23-24)

"But speaking broadly, what a writer effects by using these ornaments is to make us imagine him telling us he is a wise fellow and one that hath everything handsome about him, including a gentlemanly acquaintance with the French language." (King's English, p. 24)

In short, do not assume that, because you are writing about your French ancestors, you must splatter their native vocabulary across your pages. If you are writing in English for English-speaking readers, then you must use French only where there is no English equivalent and when you do, especially with French genealogical sources, you would do well to define your terms.

Part Eight

Dear Myrtle's Study Group on "Mastering Genealogical Proof", which we have tried to follow with steady perseverance, came to an end last Sunday, with the panellists' diligent applications of the Genealogical Proof Standard to the work of other genealogists to determine if they hold up. Based on some of the truly wacko lists of names masquerading as family genealogies that we have seen on the Internet, in certain lineage society applications and in some privately printed family histories, we think that learning to apply Dr. Jones's eleven questions (p. 95) to such works to be a fine, nay urgently needed, suggestion.

How would they be applied to comparable French genealogical publications? With difficulty, as published French genealogies do not follow the same pattern. As we have discussed earlier in this series, while North American documentation prior to the twentieth century may, for a number of reasons, be not entirely reliable -- leading, in part, to the requirement for a Genealogical Proof Standard in the first place -- that is rarely the case with French documentation. (As a matter of fact, we surmise that France's historical, busy-body approach to documenting as much as possible about everyone's private life may have been the very reason some of her citizens chose to hop a boat for what was once the Land of Opportunity and Anonymity.)

We have never seen articles concerning the genealogical proof of an ancestor's identity, such as one would find in the "National Genealogical Society Quarterly" or the "New England Historical and Genealogical Register", in French genealogical publications because the occurrence of vague or untrustworthy documentation is so rare here. Yet, mysteries as to identity abound, in most cases because a father and possibly also a mother were not named (*non dénommé*) on a birth registration or because a child was born *sous X*, or anonymously. As the birth registration in France is the core document for all subsequent documentation about a person, this can constitute a monumental brick wall.

With the advent of online genealogy and of websites where people post their family trees, a very small amount of chipping away at this type of brick wall is beginning. People descended from someone born fully or partially anonymously are putting their guesses, reasonings, suppositions about the unnamed parents into their online trees. These, we think, are one of the few types of French genealogical works that could be submitted to examination according to the Genealogical Proof Standards with useful results.

By way of example: we have been researching for some years a well-documented Parisian family - Jean-François Robert, his wife, Catherine Caroline Debanne, and their three sons -- and have explored a number of its generations. We felt ourself to be something of an expert on this family (ah, hubris) when lo, one day we were informed of a genealogy online which claimed that an ancestress, Caroline Martin, whose father was not named on her birth registration, was a daughter of the family we were studying. Briefly, the reasons for the claim were:

1. "There is no document to show that Jean-François Robert (1763-1844) may have been the father of Caroline Martin (1825-1900), wife of Victor Gassaud (1818-1868).

2. A hand-drawn genealogical chart -- now lost -- on which appeared, beside the legitimate spouse of Jean-François Robert, Catherine Caroline Debanne, and her sons, Catherine Martin, mother of Caroline.

3. Papa told me often that little Caroline was reared with the Robert boys.

4. When Caroline married Victor Gassaud in 1846, she had a large dowry. Her marriage contract specified that she had a trousseau, furniture and silver, valued at 2600 francs, 30 Belgian annuities of 50

francs, ...all "given by hand". They could only have come from her natural father.

5. Jean-François Robert's grandson was a witness, identified as a nephew, on the death registration of Caroline Martin, and at the marriage of her grandson, Henri.

6. In turn, Caroline's grandson Henri, identified as a cousin, was a witness on the death registration of the grandson of Jean-François Robert.

7. As late as the 1920s, members of the Robert family were included in the list of bereaved on the funeral announcements of the Gassaud family."

The descendant of Caroline, who gave the points we quote above did indeed have a clear research question and did cite her sources -- birth, marriage and death registrations all of which could be verified. Without question her search was exhaustive and her sources, which included notarial records in addition to the civil registrations, were excellent. Her claims based on family lore -- that there was a hand-written genealogy and that "little Caroline was reared with the Robert boys" -- could not be verified, (though it could be noted that the youngest Robert boy was nine when Caroline was born and the first Robert grandchild was born when she was nineteen, making it unlikely that she was a playmate of any of them). Nor could it be verified that the large dowry given "by hand" to Caroline, who married two years after the death of Jean-François Robert, came from him. Additionally, the descendant showed how the relationships in nos. 5 and 6 above would indeed be true were Caroline to have been the daughter of Jean-François Robert.

The descendant's conclusion is not claimed to be more than a strong suspicion. It is obvious to all that, if Caroline were his daughter, Jean-François was scrupulous in ensuring that no document with their two names should ever exist: he is not named on her birth, marriage or death registration; he is not named in her marriage contract; she is not named in his will or in the estate inventory after his death. The descendant is clearly aware that her only hope of proof would be through DNA testing with known descendants of Jean-François Robert. Her case, however, is very well made and using the Genealogical Proof Standard (albeit loosely, to allow for the many cultural differences) to examine it makes that clearer.

It was a good study group and many thanks to Dear Myrtle for organizing and presenting it.

Appendix A
INSEE Codes

Citing the sources for French records found during original research and then used in genealogy reports can be tricky. Most people begin their research with the *actes d'état civil*, the civil registrations of birth, marriage and death. These are the easiest for which to cite a source, but yet can be difficult.

In the definitive text for genealogists on the subject, *Evidence Explained*, by Elizabeth Shown Mills, the suggestion is that the source list entry should give the country, department, arrondissement, and town, in that order. Then, stating that "Worldwide, these records are more likely to be consulted via the Family History Library microfilm"' she suggests giving the FHL microfilm number as well. We suspect that users are gradually switching to the immediacy and free use of the websites of the departmental archives (see the panel to the left) in preference to the long wait for the rented FHL films. As each department seems to source differently, this can be thorny. To cite a few:

- The department of Yonne gives as the preferred sourcing: Town, Date range, film number, frame number.

- The department for Paris gives: Department name, type of *acte*, arrondissement, date, film number.

- The department of Tarn-et-Garonne gives the archives code, commune (or town) name, old town name, parish, type of registration, type of *acte*, date range

Do we respect the sourcing style of the department or do we modify it - risking their wrath, perhaps - for the sake of consistency?

The problem of sourcing changes yet again when the source is not microfilm at all but the original register. We have enormous respect for the work of Ms. Shown Mills, but wonder if we may not propose an alternative which could be used for original records.

In France, the largest administrative division is the region. Regions are divided into departments. Departments are divided into *arrondisements*, which are divided into cantons, in which are found *communes*: e.g. cities, towns, villages, hamlets, etc. Giving the full name for each can be quite long and occasionally repetitive. For example, for the village of La Chapelle-Hugon, the full address would read like this:

La Chapelle-Hugon, La Guerche-sur-l'Aubois, Saint-Amand-Montrond, Cher, Centre.

The source citation would begin like this:

France. Cher. Saint-Amand-Montrond. La Chappelle-Hugon.

This seems very unwieldy for practicality. In conversation, one would say only the town and department:

La Chapelle-Hugon, Cher.

This, however, is too short for clarity, and giving so little for sourcing would be incomplete and would lead to confusion, particularly as there are dozens of towns in France with the same name, sometimes within the same department.

French officialdom tends to use town, canton, department for a full address, which would be:

La Chapelle-Hugon, La Guerche-sur-l'Aubois, Cher

Following that lead, the full source would be:

France. Cher. La Guerche-sur-l'Aubois. La Chapelle-Hugon.

Which is every bit as unwieldy as the earlier version. When applied to large cities which are also the seats of cantons and *arrondissements*, it would be:

France. Cher. Bourges. Bourges. [and maybe another] *Bourges.*

This would be stickling to the point of silliness.

Having lived with the problem of correct identification of towns, and being a people of excellent mapping and documentation skills, the French have created a system which we would like to suggest could be used in sourcing. The national institute of statistics in France is *L'Institut national de la statistique et des études eeconomiques.*[12] INSEE, as it is known, has allotted a unique number to every town of every size in the country. For large cities, such as Paris and Lyon, which have *arrondissements* within the city, each *arrondissement* has its own code. This number, the *code commune*, (or more properly the *code officiel géographique*), is not to be confused with the postcode. A postcode may apply to a large area and be shared by many villages, whilst the INSEE code is unique. The use of the INSEE code eliminates any chance of confusion. It could also eliminate the unwieldy and unnatural use of *arrondissements* and cantons in sources. Instead, a source for an original register could begin:

France. Cher. La Chapelle-Hugon (INSEE 18048)

Could the INSEE code, we wonder, be acceptable for use to make for a briefer, yet more precise, sourcing of original records?

---

[12] http://www.insee.fr

Appendix B
Further to Citation

A year or so after the publication of this slim booklet, we wrote again on citation issues, e.g. how should genealogists working in Anglophone countries and using the citation and footnoting rules there cite French archival records? We give those two posts in this appendix.

Citing French Documents As Genealogical Sources

Dear Readers, we ask your help with citation of French documents following the principles of Elizabeth Shown Mills's "Evidence Explained: Citing History Sources from Artifacts to Cyberspace". In our Sisyphean struggle with this, you may envision us as pretty much flattened under the stone.

As per procedure, we create for each source a source note, a full reference note and a short /subsequent reference note, trying to use the suggestions and templates for French records as given in "Evidence Explained".

Here are our difficulties:

- All of our research involves the use of French documents and archives, whether originals or copies, viewed either on site at the repositories or on the websites that they operate. We do not have access to and therefore never use Family History Libraries. Yet many of the "Evidence Explained" notes concern only Family History Library copies of (sometimes) the same resource. The Family History Library source may be simply a microfilm number, while the Departmental Archive source in France may have a title in words and its own archives code or number. These surely should be included in the citation, but how?

- In giving the locations not of the documents but of their creation, particularly for parish and civil registrations and for census returns, the fact that the French civil administrative structure is quite different from that in the United States means that the two -- to our mind -- really cannot follow the same format. Additionally, the former has recently been reorganised. Allow us to explain at length:

In France, the largest administrative division is the region, the number of which were reduced in 2015 from 27 to 18. Regions are divided into departments, of which there are 101. Departments are divided into *arrondissements*, of which there are 342. In most cases, an arrondissement is also a chef-lieu, something like a county seat; but where it is not, the arrondissement is administered by a person with the title of *sous-préfet*.

Arrondissements are divided into cantons, which are not a straightforward step in the hierarchy as they were established mostly to manage services such as the local police, firemen, local elections and - please note - census taking. Confusingly, a commune that is a large city can have many cantons, while a canton in the countryside may encompass many communes. In 2013, France had 4055 cantons.

Arrondissements are also divided into *communes*, the primary administrative level, created in 1789 from what had been church parishes. A *commune* may be a city, town, or village. A *commune* will have a mayor, a municipal council and, crucially here, the responsibility for the civil registration of births, marriages and deaths within its boundaries. Since the re-organisation of 2015, some but not all *communes* have been grouped into intercommunalities, to share administrative services and responsibilities. France currently has 35,585 *communes*.

These hierarchical divisions of territorial administration are, in descending order:

Region-department-arrondissement-[canton]-commune

However, for a large city like Paris, the commune of France with the highest population, it can look like this:

Region-department-metropolitan commune-arrondissement

Since 1964, Paris -- ever the oddball -- has been both a *commune* and a department, divided into 20 *arrondissements* which are also cantons, so an example of the above hierarchy might be written as:

Ile-de-France - Paris - 9th *arrondissement*

In Paris, Lyon and Marseille, the civil registration is carried out at the *arrondissement* level. In this case, an *arrondissement* is comparable to a borough in New York City or London (but imagine that New York City also had a borough named New York). At the same time, in the more general use across the rest of the country, an *arrondissement* is similar to a county within an American state or to a borough or district within a British county.

Trying to make this varied administrative structure, with different terms occupying different places in the hierarchy at the same time, fit into a single and rigid citation structure has proved nearly impossible for us. Nor can we always craft a citation that can fit with the recommendations for French sources in "Evidence Explained".

We would like to propose a couple of things, to begin with, at least:

- Because of the way that a term, such as *arrondissement*, can indicate more than one function or administrative level, and because a level of administration, such as a canton, can be in a higher or lower position, the function of places should perhaps be stated in the full reference note, thus, instead of the location part of a census note reading:

•

Saint-Martin-Choquel, Desvres, Boulogne-sur-Mer, Pas-de-Calais

it would read:

Saint-Martin-Choquel [*code commune*: 62759], *canton de* Desvres, *arrondissement de* Boulogne-sur-Mer, *département du* Pas-de-Calais

But, it has to be said that the above, though more clear, is a bit heavy. And what to do when, as with Boulogne-sur-Mer, the place is *commune*, canton and *arrondissement* all at once?

• The *code commune* is something we like for two reasons:

1) It really is a lifesaver in eliminating confusion. Because France has numerous *communes* of the same name, such as Saint Martin, the *code commune* is the only unique identifier. (See Appendix A) On the French pages of wikipedia, every *commune* is given, showing its *code commune* as well as what are its intercommunality, canton, *arrondissement*, department and region. One can type in the search box just the code and any garbled version of the *commune* name and, usually, the correct page will come up. The same is true of the French GeneaWiki website. So, we would like to suggest that, at least once, in one note or another, it be given in brackets.

2) The *commune*, not the canton or arrondissement, is the key location to know in searching for or identifying the provenance of most French civil records relating to individuals, so it, above all, has to be clearly identified. (More on this below.)

• It is crucial that the name of the *commune* be given in every note. In France, few records are created or arranged at the *arrondissement* level in the way that

US records may be arranged at the county level. EVERYTHING concerning civil registrations is organised from the *commune* level, as that is where the registers are created, in duplicate, and where one set is stored. So, any note that shows only an *arrondissement* and a department, but not the commune, leaves us profoundly uncomfortable. A short/subsequent note would more closely follow French custom if it gave the *commune* and department only.

Census returns also are created with the identification on the front page showing:

commune-canton-arrondissement-department

(the last usually being pre-printed).

They are retrieved/arranged online by *commune* name as well. Again, it would make sense for a shorter note to leave out an *arrondissement* and/or canton name but never, ever omit the *commune* name.

- Really, also, we wonder about the title used for parish and civil registrations. Instead of a generic term that seems to come from the Family History Library microfilms, ("*États-civil*", which is also ungrammatical) when we are using the copies on the websites of the Departmental Archives or other repositories, shouldn't we be using the series titles given there? For example:

    - "*Registres paroissiaux et d'état civil*" on the websites of the ADs of Pas-de-Calais, Aveyron and many others

    - "*Registres paroissiaux, pastoraux et d'état civil*" on the website of the AD of Charente-Maritime

    - "*Etat Civil Numérisé des Origines à 1932*" on the website of the AD of Cantal

    - "*Registres paroissiaux et documents d'état civil*" on the website of the AD of Bas-Rhin

- *"Etat civil et tables décennales (1501-1932)"* on the website of the AD of Savoie

In addition to he above, which mostly applies to parish and civil registrations and census returns, there are the military lists which can be found on almost every Departmental Archives website and which many of us use as sources.

Military recruitment lists from the nineteenth century onwards are something used a great deal in French genealogy as they provide many details about an individual, and as so many men emigrated from France when their 20th birthday drew near. Most are now accessible online, or at least the indices to them are. They were created in and are arranged according to recruitment bureaux.

These bureaux are in a military hierarchy of administration and geography that have little to do with the civil structure outlined above. There were created, in 1874, nineteen military recruitment regions, the largest category in the structure; there have been alterations since then. Their numbers have no relationship whatsoever to the numbers given to French departments, which are given in alphabetical order; but correspond to the regions covered by the different French Army corps. Each region was given eight subdivisions of bureaux; these were located in selected but not all *arrondissements* or cantons, the selection having been based on population. The archives of the bureaux are stored in the Departmental Archives where the bureau was located.

We would suggest that the reference note concerning these give, in addition to the department, the bureau location which, again, could be indicated as something like *"bureau de"* or *"bureau de recrutement de"*, but not attempt to follow the civil hierarchical structure.

As to French resources on the subject of citation, we have found precious few. One of the clearest is a blog by a history professor at Lille, one Emilien Ruiz, entitled *"Devenir historien-ne"*, and specifically the post *"Comment citer un document d'archives, une thèse ou un mémoire ?".*[13] About half-way down that post, under the heading *"Citer un document d'archives"*, Professor Ruiz gives a very clear explanation of *notes de bas de page* (e.g. full reference notes) and *notes en annexe "Sources et bibliographie"* (e.g. source list entry notes). However, his examples do not include precisely the document types of concern here.

---

[13] http://devhist.hypotheses.org/1215

Further To Citation Issues

Continuing our research into how better to cite French genealogy documents and sources for our discussion with Elizabeth Shown Mills, author of "Evidence Explained: : Citing History Sources from Artifacts to Cyberspace".¹ (who is most generously offering her encouragement in this effort) we have been trawling the blogs of various French experts.

Roland B. writes that he gives:

- The type of record series or group, e.g. "BMS" for a parish registration or "*état civil*" for a civil registration or "*acte notarié*" for a notarial record.

- The place of provenance, which he gives as the department number only and then the *commune* name in capitals, e.g. "28 ILLIERS" or "41 LANCE"

- The year the document was created

- The specific type of document, e.g. "*contrat mariage*" or "*décès*"

- The name(s) of the individual(s) in the document, with the surname in capitals

Thus, his list of citation examples includes:

- *Acte notarié>1822 Contrat mariage : André FALBET et Maria CASTAIGNÉ*

- *BMS 28 ILLIERS>1788 mariage : CHATEAU Hilarion & GROSSET Marie Louise*

- *Etat civil 41 LANCE>1895 décès : MOYER Marie Louise* ¹⁴

---

¹⁴ B., Roland, "*Les Sources en généalogie*" Web log post, Lorand.org, 17 April 2012, (http://www.lorand.org/spip.php?article157), accessed 21 November 2016.

When compared with the requirements given in "Evidence Explained", these seem not to contain enough information. Here is what Ms. Mills says is required for a citation of "Derivatives & Imaged Sources", which is what microfilms of parish and civil registers as viewed on the websites of Departmental Archives are :

- "distinguish between image copies and other derivatives; such as abstracts, transcripts, and information extracted into databases;
- credit properly the original creator;
- credit properly the producer of the film or electronic publication;
- identify clearly the nature of the material;
- identify the film or electronic publications completely enough for others to locate it;
- cite the specific place (page, frame, etc.) on the roll, fiche, or database at which we found the relevant detail; and
- cite the date on which the microfilm or electronic data set was created (if that information is provided), updated, or accessed - as well as the date of the relevant record."[15]

Thus, for a full reference note on the Departmental Archive copy of a burial in a parish register, "Evidence Explained" gives:

> "Saint-Nicolas Parish (*Saint-Nicolas, Diocese of Coutances*), Burial Register, 1769-1791, p. 339, Marie Lemiére burial (1771); microfilm 1Mi EC26, roll 11; *Archives Départementales de la Manche*, St.-Lo, France."[16]

There is an extremely long and interesting discussion of how one should cite French sources on the blog of Sophie

---

[15] Mills, "Evidence Explained", p.47.

[16] Ibid., p.357.

Boudarel, *"La Gazette des Ancêtres"*.[17] Each commenter has contributed his or her own personal style, many of which lean toward something that is completely in numerical codes. The discussion is exclusively on how to create what "Evidence Explained" terms a "source list entry"; there is no discussion at all on how to cite a source which is a parish or civil registration in a reference note or footnote. This makes it impossible to compare any French reference note or footnote for this type of documentation with the style recommended in "Evidence Explained". Language differences and translations aside, would French genealogists require more for the online version of the record cited above? And, if so, what exactly?

The same is true for the French Geneawiki page[18] on the subject: there is no standard format recommended for a source list entry or its equivalent, and there is no discussion at all of crafting reference notes or footnotes for sources. There is, however, much discussion of the need to separate the idea of a source from the information it contains, which is comparable to the explanation of the primary and secondary information a source may contain in "Evidence Explained".[19]

We will continue this investigation with, we hope, discussions with archivists and historians, for the genealogy community here in France would seem to be addressing different issues.

---

[17] Boudarel, Sophie, "Comment nommer ses documents en généalogie?", Web log post, Blogspot.fr, 18 April 2012, (http://lagazettedesancetres.blogspot.fr/2012/04/comment-nommer-ses-sources-en.html), accessed 23 November 2016.

[18] *"Terminologie : Source ou citation de source?"* Web site page, Geneawiki.com, updated 2 November 2016, (https://fr.geneawiki.com/index.php/A_quoi_servent_les_sources_%3F #Terminologie_:_Source_ou_citation_de_source_.3F), accessed 23 November 2016.

[19] Mills, "Evidence Explained", pp.24-25.